Marriage That Works

Is Work

June 23, 2019
Dear Dengel & Bianca
Mrs Harper and I cannot do
Personal Marriage Counseling
for You But this Book was
By
Written By a good Friend of
James Rudy Gray, BA, MA, Th.M., D.Min.
Ours. Read it and Share
What you are learning.

Ephesians 5:21 - 6:4

Bro and Sisten Harper

1

Marriage That Works Is Work

Copyright 2007 by James R. Gray
ISBN 978-1-4276-2245-7

My wife and I lovingly dedicate this book
To our three precious daughters, Becky,
Katy, and Cindy.

Preface

Marriage is a human relationship designed by God. In this potentially great partnership between a man, a woman, and God, failure too often occurs. A couple gets married with the expectation that it will last for a lifetime. Most probably expect a happy experience. What our high divorce rate reflects is that marriage is hard work. It takes commitment to God and to our mate. It involves knowing and accepting who we are and who we married. It includes growing to appreciate the differences that exist between us.

The hard work is not getting married. That is relatively easy in our society. The hard work is building a relationship that works. In this kind of marriage, several things become focal points for our dedicated effort: growing in intimacy, communicating effectively, understanding personality, birth order, and gender differences, enjoying and controlling the power of human sexuality, realizing the significance of money, and learning to be friends.

I have been a pastor for over 30 years. I have also worked as a Christian counselor for many of those years. For over 20 years, my wife and I have conducted marriage enrichment retreats. The work before you is the result of those years as a minister, counselor, seminar leader, and husband. Over the years, I have discovered some basic keys that seem to unlock the passage for building a strong and healthy marriage. Please don't get me wrong. Building a good and Godly marriage takes work. However, it is not simply *that* we work at our marriages but *how* we work at them. We can work harder or we can work smarter. No marriage will ever be perfect, but a marriage where two people know Christ, believe His Word, and love each other can work --- if husband and wife are willing to do the work it takes.

My wife and I pray that this book may be a tool in God's hands to bring health and strength to your marriage as you work at it together for His glory and the good of your marriage.

James Rudy Gray

Chapter 1

Designed For Intimacy

Intimacy is God's design for marriage. After creating man and woman, God said in Genesis 2:24, "For this cause a man shall leave his father and his mother, and shall cleave to his wife; and they shall become one flesh." This verse is quoted in Matt 19:4-6, Mark 10:7-8, I Cor. 6:16, and Eph. 5:31. The one-flesh experience is intimacy. It certainly refers to the sexual union between a man and a woman but it includes more.

Spiritual intimacy where a husband and wife actually share the things of God together is the most important and highest level of intimacy a couple can achieve. It is more than simply attending church together or having Christian values in common. It is actively and deliberately sharing a relationship with God together. It may include prayer, service, church work, child rearing, benevolence work, evangelistic work, etc. This type of intimacy shares thoughts and feelings of God and His truth with your mate through a disposition of trust, openness, and integrity.

Sexual intimacy is also a very important part of building an intimate marriage. More than sexual intercourse, it involves the sharing of our male and female sexuality with each other. We could think of sex as what we do and sexuality as who we are.

According to Howard and Charlotte Clinebell there are at least 10 dimensions of intimacy. In addition to spiritual and sexual intimacy, these are emotional, intellectual, aesthetic, creative, recreational, work, crisis, and commitment.[1] Others could likely be added to this list. The concept to grasp is that intimacy is much broader than we typically think. It is about sharing a life together.

The word intimacy implies familiarity, innermost, private, and personal. Being intimate with your mate involves growing in your understanding of the inner reality of that person. An intimate marriage is one where two people risk sharing who they are with their mate and genuinely receive the reality shared by the other spouse. In the process of knowing our mate and being known by them, we also discover more about ourselves. Intimacy is nurtured through mutual acceptance and appreciation.

If intimacy is the design for marriage then commitment to Christ, His Word, and our spouse is the foundation. From that foundation, we can build a marriage that works. The blessings are many and the challenges are real. Difficulties are certain to arise. Disappointments and even tragedies may come. But when a marriage is working according to God's design, the experience of intimacy will be real. Happiness is not the goal of marriage. Godliness is. When we grow personally as Christ's followers and build a marriage empowered by His truth, we will discover the joy and blessing that only the mystery of marriage can provide. Married people can be happy. But happiness is a by-product of a specific life direction or commitment. An example of this in Scripture is found in Matthew 6:33, "Seek first His Kingdom and His righteousness, and all these things will be added to you."

Commitment is perhaps the best way to understand love. The Greeks had four words that we translate into English as love. Three of the four occur in the New Testament, but only one is the love that can build a marriage. Agape is the Greek word for love used numerous times throughout the New Testament. This Greek word for love is an attitude that seeks to do what is best and right and the action of doing it sacrificially and unconditionally. The sum total of all the commandments is to love God. The second is like it: love your neighbor. A neighbor is anyone God places in the path of your life that you can help. Your mate is your number one neighbor.

Agape love is not an emotional word. In each of the following verses, it is agape that is used. We are commanded to love God and love our neighbor (Matt. 22:37-39), love our enemies (Matt. 5:44), love one another (John 15:12), and love our wives (Eph. 5:25). God so loved the world that He sent Jesus to die in our place on the cross (John 3:16). God did not simply have warm and tender feelings for the world, He did something that was good and right, and He did it sacrificially and unconditionally. Believers are reminded in Romans 5:5 that "the love of God has been poured out within our hearts through the Holy Spirit who was given to us." Galatians 5:22 tells us that the fruit of the Spirit is love..." I John 4:7-8 makes the origin in us very clear, "... love is from God; and everyone who loves us is born of God and knows God. The one who does not love does not know God, for God is love." I John 4:19 drives the point home with unmistakable clarity, "We love, because He first loved us."

Intimacy in marriage is the result of commitment at work. Commitment is love and this kind of love comes from God. We are capable of loving this way, but only by yielding to the Spirit of God who resides in the life of every born again person. I Corinthians 13:4-7 does not define agape but it does describe this kind of love for us. "Love is

9

patient, love is kind and is not jealous; love does not brag and is not arrogant, does not act unbecomingly; it does not seek its own, is not provoked, does not take into account a wrong suffered, does not rejoice in unrighteousness, but rejoices with the truth; bears all things, believes all things, hopes all things, endures all things."

Any discussion of love in our society, conjures up ideas of feelings. Feelings follow thoughts. We have feelings because we have thoughts. Good feelings will also follow agape. But, even if good feelings did not follow agape, this kind of love is good and better than our best feelings. God has given us our emotions, and they are good. But our feelings cannot be the basis of how we build our lives or our marriages. Only His truth will provide the wisdom, power, and longevity to build a strong marriage.

Every relationship between a man and woman begins with infatuation. Strong feelings of attraction and romance run high during this experience. It has been described as exhilarating. Some psychologists have compared this state to thinking and feeling like a manic person. Others have seen similarities between infatuation and addiction. Unless a relationship grows beyond the infatuation stage and into a more mature love, that relationship has little chance of surviving, yet alone thriving.

There are three general descriptions that can be applied to marriages. An enmeshed marriage is one where a husband and wife are living in a co-dependent existence. They have convinced themselves that they need each other in order to complete themselves. As a result their personal boundaries are so blurred that they don't seem to be able to function without each other. This type of marriage is unhealthy and in need of significant change if any degree of health is to be achieved. A husband or wife can never complete the other person. We are designed by God to complement each other but only God can complete a person's life. In the enmeshed marriage, there is too much closeness or togetherness. One marriage counselor tells his pre-marital clients, "You are not ready to live with each other until you know you can live without each other."

Another type of possible marriage is the disengaged marriage where there is too much distance between the two. In fact, it is almost as though two single people share a living space. One wife was overheard to say, "My husband and I get along great now. He just goes his way and does his own thing, and I do the same. We hardly ever see each other, but we never fight." That is descriptive of a disengaged marriage. In this type of relationship the couple lives with too much separate identity and not nearly enough togetherness. Our relationships do become a part of us in healthy personal development. If a genuine sense of "us" or "we" is not developed in the marriage, that marriage cannot succeed even if the couple remains legally married. In fact, one of the ways that we build intimate memories is by doing things together. One of the reasons those memories are made is because we spend enough time apart to want to build the memories together.

Both the disengaged and the enmeshed marriage are models of failure. They can be changed, but not without God's grace and hard work by both husband and wife.

The third type of marriage is an intimate marriage. This is God's design for us. It involves leaving our family of origin and establishing a new life and home with our spouse. It means deliberately being an individual and at the same time sharing an ongoing commitment to the other person. It is togetherness without co-dependency and separateness without becoming disengaged. It is the balance between too much apartness and too much togetherness. The Bible presents intimacy as the process of becoming one and yet maintaining our unique personality and individuality. In John 10:30, Jesus said, "I and the Father are one." The trinity is a mystery and a reality. God is one. Yet God exists in three distinct persons. Intimacy, in a less complicated fashion, is somewhat like this. We are one in relationship but we maintain our separate personalities. It is that dynamic of being one-flesh yet remaining as two distinct people that allows us the power to build intimacy.

One of the major obstacles many couples face in building a strong Christian marriage is a bad start. Two chief objectives of the adolescent period in life is to achieve an identity and establish independence. When these are not met, the results will be evident in an immature marriage. We know that adolescence begins with puberty but it is debatable when it ends. Some psychologists have suggested that adolescence concludes when the young adult has reached financial independence. If that is the case, it is possible to have 40 year old adolescents today! Some experts believe that it may take about 10 years of marriage before a couple can really develop intimacy. Then it will grow and develop only with hard work. Building intimacy in marriage is hard work but it is God's work for us as husbands and wives. We can certainly begin to grow in intimacy early in our marriage, if we start well and continue with the kind of faith that is genuine and Biblical. Preparation precedes blessing in most any endeavor in life. This is certainly true of marriage. While we will change, grow, and develop as individuals and as a couple, we can have a successful marriage without several years of trial and error. Our failures, however, do not destroy intimacy. In fact marital intimacy is often built on the ashes of mistakes. Forgiveness is a vital force in any marriage. Ephesians 4:32 says, "Be kind to one another, tender-hearted, forgiving each other, just as God in Christ also has forgiven you." As human beings who live in a world that is still under the curse of sin, we will see the affects of that in every person, organization, institution, relationship, government, business, and church. We will fail but we do not have to be failures. We have not failed at intimacy if we have messed up. We have failed when we give up and quit. As long as intimacy is our goal and we are dedicated to using the resources of God to achieve it, we can continue to grow in intimacy.

The goal of marriage is intimacy, but that experience of intimacy is expressed in a variety of ways among couples. No two healthy marriages will look alike, but they will share many of the same characteristics. One of the interesting ways we can determine how well we are progressing in our intimacy is to examine our conflicts. All couples disagree. In fact, it is better for parents to let their kids see them disagree and make up than it is to never let their children see them argue at all. This way kids grow up knowing the reality of conflict and the importance of conflict resolution. That we have conflict is not necessarily a negative thing. *What* we argue about is not as important as most of us probably believe. The key is *how* we disagree. An intimate marriage allows us the confidence and assurance to disagree without damaging the relationship or alienating our mate.

Differences can actually help us build intimacy if we are more concerned with creating harmony than playing a solo. The art of compromise is the golden rule in the marriage relationship. Accepting your mate is not the same thing as acknowledging them. Accepting them is actually demonstrating to them that you care and that you want them to have the freedom to develop personally.

By spending some time apart, we are drawn to spend more time together. The old adage has merit, "Absence makes the heart grow fonder." Togetherness with a healthy separateness is the principle to remember. Being able to be who we are is essential in building intimacy. However, we will not feel the freedom to be who we are until we are accepted for who we are by our mate. We are less fearful and more confident when the people we know and love accept us. In that type of environment, we can be more vulnerable and reveal more of ourselves. This sharing of our hearts is fundamental to growing in intimacy.

One of the basic needs of a human being is the need to be appreciated. When we live in intimacy with our spouse we show them appreciation and accept his or her expressions of appreciation to us. Intimacy, like compatibility, does not mean we are alike but that we know who we are and who our mate is. From that understanding we seek to make meaningful connections and build a relationship around mutuality rather than self-satisfying endeavors.

Every relationship that has health and vitality also has some mystery. Intimacy does not attempt to define all the mysteries in a relationship, but chooses to affirm and embrace the mysteries in a positive and trusting way. Secrets that damage or corrupt the relationship are bad, but mystery exists in most relationships. A state of intimacy is not threatened by the presence of what is not known. Mystery exists in most relationships, but in an intimate marriage it is more celebrated than feared. Intimacy means sharing our true inner selves with each other, but it does not mean we need to share everything. For some personality types that would be virtually impossible. Should a husband and wife tell each other everything? Husbands and wives should be honest with each other, but the purpose of sharing our hearts is not simply to clear our conscience but to build intimacy with our mate and not create division and hurt.

One of the most common illusions about intimacy is the mistaken idea that it is either easy or magical. It is hard work. Intimacy is the design of God for marriage that overcomes the basic conflict that seems to threaten marriage: the need for closeness and at the same time the fear of closeness. Intimacy is the experience of balanced living in the covenant of marriage. It is truly a oneness with a healthy togetherness.

There can be no intimacy without sharing. The level and method of sharing will vary from couple to couple, but the fact of sharing heart to heart will be present in each intimate marriage. One dangerous pitfall in sharing is sharing without restraint. We can speak our mind or give our opinion and actually hinder rather than build intimacy. Restraint of selfish and destructive sharing is also an expression of intimacy. It is not that we never share negative or even critical things, but that we never share them in selfish or vindictive ways. Love does not tear down, it builds up. Love shows our mates we value them. Intimacy does not run on the fuel of selfishness or evil. It operates out of the principle found in Ephesians 4:15, "speaking the truth in love."

Intimacy building does not lead to intentional injury or insult but to focused caring and encouragement. It does not avoid the unpleasant, but deals with it in a way that provides both support and understanding. Living out intimacy means being devoted to living in a manner that strives to help the other person feel better and be better as a person and as a mate. The one-flesh relationship is the glue that keeps a couple flourishing in the different seasons of life.

There are some practical hurdles to building intimacy that occur: lack of time, fear of rejection, low self-esteem, emotional immaturity, unreal expectations, selfishness, anger, inattention, misplaced priorities, lack of involvement, and others. In order to overcome these obstacles and build intimacy a couple needs to be willing to be open and honest; have realistic expectations; practice both commitment and acceptance; and seek the spouse's well being.

Lust can be a major roadblock toward intimacy. Women have a tendency to lust regarding the romantic aspects of a relationship while men seem to be more prone to physical and sexual lust. Lust is an inordinate desire for something. Desire is good, but lust is desire gone too far. Intimacy cannot grow in a climate of lust, but it will prosper in hearts of true devotion to God and each other.

Intimacy is God's design for marriage. He made us with the capability to enjoy it and in so doing become an illustration of Christ and His bride, the church. Intimacy is the goal of marriage and commitment is the foundation upon which intimacy is realized.

Chapter 2
My Personality Type

The idea of temperament or personality type goes back hundreds of years.

Carl Jung developed a model for classifying people according to eight personality types. Katherine Briggs and her daughter Isabel Briggs Meyers later built on the work of Jung and enlarged the theory to include 16 types. The result of their research was the development of a questionnaire for measuring personality type called the Myers-Briggs Type Indicator. The MBTI is one of the leading instruments used to measure personality type today.

What follows is a brief personality preference questionnaire that can help you discover more about your particular type. The theory is that each person has a personality type, a four-letter identification that reveals some important generalities about a person. For a more detailed and professional analysis, you should contact a professional counselor who can administer the MBTI.

In each of the four sections of questions given below, please circle the number one or two in each pair of options that best describes you. When you are finished with each section, count the number of one's and two's you circled and enter that number beside the letter in the preference profile. You will have a four-letter type that reflects your preferences. After determining what your four-letter type is, read the descriptions of the sixteen types that are given.

Section One
1. Are you more likely to:
    1. Talk with many people at a gathering.
    2. Speak with a few people who you know
2. Do you tend to:
    1. Think out loud
    2. Think things through before talking
3. Do you have:
    1. Many friends and acquaintances.
    2. A few friends
4. In a social setting are you more likely to:
    1. Actively engage in conversation
    2. Enjoy listening more than talking
5. Would people who know you say you are:
    1. Approachable.
    2. Reserved or Shy
6. In the presence of others, do you tend to be:
    1. An initiator
    2. A Responder
7. When you interact with people does it:
    1. Energize and motivate you
    2. Tire and drain you
8. When the door bell rings, are you more likely to think:
    1. Oh boy!
    2. Oh no!
9. Do you come across as more:
    1. Outgoing
    2. Private

10. Are you more often:
    1. Introducing others
    2. Being introduced by others
11. Which do you prefer:
    1. Interacting with people
    2. Reading a book, etc.

Put the number of 1's circled in this space: 1's_____
Put the number of 2's circled in this space: 2's_____

Section Two
1. Are you more:
   1. Practical
   2. Creative
2. Are you better at:
   1. Managing what exists
   2. Designing something new
3. What kind of people do you prefer:
   1. Sensible types
   2. Imaginative types
4. Are you more oriented toward:
   1. The present
   2. The future
5. Is your thinking influenced more by:
   1. The facts
   2. The possibilities
6. Do you prefer what is:
   1. Actual
   2. Potential
7. On a work project, which is more like you:
   1. Do it according to plans and procedures
   2. Do it your way
8. In speaking, are you typically:
   1. Literal and straight-forward
   2. Symbolic and descriptive

9. Would you describe your thinking style as:
    1. Concrete
    2. Abstract
10. When making decisions, which are you more likely to depend on:
    1. Facts and prior experience
    2. A feeling or a hunch
11. Are you more:
    1. Interested in details
    2. Focused on the big picture

Put the number of 1's circled in this space: 1's_____
Put the number of 2's circled in this space: 2's_____

Section Three

1. Are you more:
    1. Objective
    2. Tolerant
2. Is it more important for you to:
    1. Do what you believe is right
    2. Create harmony and avoid conflict
3. Would you most likely decide something by:
    1. Being convinced by facts
    2. Being moved by your emotions
4. What is more important:
    1. Principles
    2. Circumstances
5. Which do you value the most:
    1. Reason and logic
    2. Affection and concern
6. Would you consider yourself a:
    1. Fair-minded person
    2. Warm-hearted person

7. What word best describes how you choose:
    1. Think
    2. Feel
  8. Would you rather be:
    1. Competent
    2. Likeable
  9. What is more valuable to you:
    1. Truth and justice
    2. Mercy and compassion
  10. Would you rather be regarded as:
    1. A person of conviction
    2. A caring person
  11. What is typically your first reaction to something:
    1. See what's wrong
    2. Appreciate

Put the number of 1's circled in this space: 1's_____
Put the number of 2's circled in this space: 2's_____

Section Four

  1. Do you prefer to:
    1. Organize and plan for things
    2. Go with the flow
  2. Are you more:
    1. Structured
    2. Spontaneous
  3. Do you like a work environment that is:
    1. Professional
    2. Casual
  4. Are you more comfortable with:
    1. Making closure
    2. Leaving your options open
  5. When planning a vacation what appeals to you most:
    1. The destination
    2. The trip and the destination

6. Are you more:
   1. Focused
   2. Easily distracted
7. When you are surprised, are you more likely to:
   1. Feel uncomfortable
   2. Like it
8. Do you prefer:
   1. Consistency
   2. Variety
9. Would you regard yourself as:
   1. Neat
   2. More messy than organized
10. Do you like to:
    1. Have control over things
    2. Just experience things
11. Are you more:
    1. Orderly and decisive
    2. Spontaneous and open

Put the number of 1's circled in this space: 1's_____
Put the number of 2's circled in this space: 2's_____

Total the numbers circled in each section:

Section One
1. (E) _____   2. (I) _____

Section Two
1. (S)_____   2. (N) _____

Section Three
1. (T) _____   2. (F) _____

Section Four
1. (J) _____   2. (P)_____

Each number is equal to the letter beside it. E = Extraversion. I = Introversion. S = Sensing. N = Intuition (N is used because I was used to represent introversion). F = Feeling. T = Thinking. J = Judging. P = Perceiving. Take the highest number in each pair of letters: (E or I, S or N, F or T, and J or P). This will give you a four letter type: ____ _____ _____ _____. There are sixteen possible types.

There are four pairs of preferences. From these come 16 possible personality types. A personality type is not a predictor of behavior, work performance, marriage compatibility, IQ, personal competence, etc. It is a personality indicator that is very helpful in understanding the general framework of a person.

ESTJ – are administrator types. They believe something worth doing, is worth doing right. They are logical, focused, disciplined, and organized. Their strength is managing in the present tense. Because they like to be decisive, they can run the risk of making decisions too hastily. They are realistic and like involvements where the results can be measured. This type is made stronger and more balanced when they learn to listen to others and express appreciation.

ESTP – are realistic and action-oriented. The sensing function takes the lead in this type. They are both curious and adaptable. As a rule, they provide good company and usually have fun with life. Because of their need for activity, they seem to need stimulating people, thoughts, and environments. They may choose to enjoy a good time rather than stick with a project until it is completed. They use the thinking function to apply rules and procedures in innovative ways. They enjoy life and are often very interested in sports or physical activities.

ESFJ – find fulfillment in being a hosts or hostesses. They are concerned about harmonious relationships and seem to radiate sympathy and tolerance. Indifference or criticism from others is hurtful to them whereas encouragement is a valuable and uplifting experience for them. They may have many personal rules and guidelines but have an innate ability to deal with people. Admitting the presence of problems or acknowledging the truth of difficulties with others is a weakness they often have. They are usually popular, outgoing people who attract people to themselves.

ESFP – can be described as friendly, outgoing, fun-loving, adaptable, tolerant and realistic. They believe in getting the most out of life that is possible. They are naturally optimistic and use their ability to adjust and adapt to meet challenges and problems. They can be both high-spirited and materialistic. Because they are highly sociable, they can be the life of the party. This type is a people-person type often very good at conflict resolution.

ENTJ – will run whatever part of the world they are given to run. They tend to be leaders who are good at long-range planning and goal-setting. This type finds work both meaningful and purposeful. They like to see what can be done and work to find ways to do it. Because they rely heavily on reason and logic, they often do not consider the feelings of other people enough. Their strength lies in seeing the big picture and they can overlook details in the process.

ENTP – like challenge and excitement. They are gifted at understanding rather than judging people and often use this to build support for themselves and their projects. This type does not enjoy routine and thrives on one project after another. They are good at starting things but may not follow through or finish what they start. They enjoy novelty and are drawn to more risk-taking types of activities and unique experiences.

ENFJ – are sympathetic people. They are friendly, tactful, sensitive, and peace-loving people. They work cooperatively with others and find great personal satisfaction in creating a harmonious environment for the people with whom they work or live. They like to have things settled, but they often prefer that others make the decisions. They think best when they are allowed to think out loud. They typically make decisions that are based on their personal values and feelings.

ENFP – enjoy seeing the possibilities that exist in doing things differently. They are innovative, creative, and imaginative. They enjoy spontaneity and freedom but become bored with routine. In various types of settings, they are invariably people-focused. They like to have fun and need stimulation. They often bring play into the work environment and humor into relationships. They may have difficulty dealing with details etc, that do not involve people.

ISTJ – have the gift of critical thought. They will usually see what is wrong with something before they can appreciate what is good about it. They are dependable, fact-oriented, practical, realistic, and responsible. This is the stable type that brings that stability to relationships, work, leisure, etc. They master details but do not promote themselves. Many will be solitary type people who enjoy time alone. They do not trust intuition and imagination and tend to feel uncomfortable with spontaneity. Duty is a big concept in their lives, and they believe in doing the job they have been given to do.

ISTP – will be convinced of something based on solid reasoning and legitimate and solid facts. They are gifted at organizing facts and data but do not like organizing people. Because they are so driven by the thinking function, they can fail to recognize and face their own feelings or even the feelings of others. They are usually very quiet and reserved but very curious. They are skilled at bringing order out of unorganized facts and find it easy to detect when something is wrong.

ISFJ – are behind-the-scenes people who are willing to accept duties and responsibilities that go beyond what is required. They have strong emotional reactions, but these feelings are rarely seen by others. They are typically hard-working, conscientious, patient, and accurate when dealing with details. Because they have good organizational skills and care about the people around them, they can be good supervisors. At home, they are most often devoted to those people they love. As a rule, they follow through with projects and seldom quit before a task is completed.

ISFP – warmth, flexibility, loyalty, and ideas govern this type. They express their feelings primarily with actions rather than words. They are faithful to the duties they have been given and to the people they care about. Jobs that provide a purpose beyond a salary are the type of work that most motivates them. They are modest and have a tendency to be somewhat self-effacing. They enjoy quiet, relaxed, and friendly atmospheres where they can express their ideals and care for others.

INTJ – live in their inner world of thoughts and ideas. They are driven to accomplish their goals and often push others to achieve with the same intensity. Because they are so goal-oriented, they need counsel and insight from others to give them a more balanced approach. They are strong thinkers who can be helped by facing and identifying their own feelings and recognizing the feelings of others. They believe virtually anything can be improved. They work diligently to master anything that is important to them. Since they have such strong analytical tendencies, they can improve their relationship abilities by learning to express feelings and appreciation.

INTP – are idea-focused and not strongly people-oriented. Their social group of friends is usually small and they enjoy being with people who enjoy discussing ideas and concepts that interest them. They are able to look beyond the present situation of something and see the potential that exists. Given to more abstract thinking, they often do well in science, math, research, etc. Because they want to state the facts in such a precise way, they can overlook the thoughts and feelings of others. They can also present an idea in such a complicated and detailed way that others may not follow. By getting in touch with their own feelings and learning to respect the feelings of others, they can enhance their own relationship skills.

INFJ – are led by the inspirations that come to them from their sixth sense, intuition. They enjoy things like reading, music, and more solitary type activities. They are not as comfortable with physical activities but feel more confident in small, intimate gatherings. They are possibility-driven and people-inspired. When they lead, they do it by winning others rather than through demanding allegiance. They approach almost any problem situation as an opportunity to find a solution. They like freedom and are stifled when regulated to a mundane routine. They show interest in new ideas and can find a rewarding life in a variety of circumstances.

INFP – usually keep their warm feelings inside. Their view of life is usually very personal, and they are motivated the most by their inner world of thoughts, ideals, and personal values. They stick to the ideals and passions they care deeply about and are loyal to the people who mean the most to them. People who show an interest in their ideals and goals are the ones INFPs cherish the most. They are usually reserved and their deepest feelings are seldom shared. They are, as a rule, open and adaptable, but can become very stubborn when their inner ideals are threatened. They can feel inadequate because of the contrast between their ideals and their accomplishments. They can become overly sensitive and lose confidence in themselves.

Chapter 3
Personalities At Work

Are we the way we are by genetic predisposition (nature) or by life conditioning (nurture)? Probably both. However, it seems that our basic personality type is the gift of our Creator. We then grow, change, and develop around that fundamental personal style throughout our life. The theory is that personality type does not change over time. In fact, we are told that as we grow older, we also grow stronger in our preferences.

An exercise that may help you relate to personality type is to sign your name as you normally do on the following   line_____.
Now   sign   your   name   using   your   opposite hand_____.   Usually what happens is that when you write with your preferred hand it feels natural, unstrained, uncomplicated, and easily legible.   When you switch to the other hand it seems strained, unnatural and requires both concentration and effort to write.   Even with focused concentration, the writing feels awkward and hardly looks legible.   Right handed people prefer using their right hand but they can use their left hand – just not as well.   It is not their preference.

Everyone uses all eight of the personality preferences (extraversion and introversion; sensing and intuition; thinking and feeling; judging and perceiving). Even though we use all eight, we will have a preference of one over the other in each pair. The four preferred functions become our personality type.

The Apostle Paul is an outstanding example of how a person becomes a new creature in Christ through the new birth and yet retains the creation gift of personality type. Paul was a hard-charging, type- A, driven, intelligent, hard-working, goal-focused Pharisee. He was so zealous in his religion that he was in charge of persecuting Christians even having some put to death. When he was blinded on the Damascus Road by the risen Christ and was born again, life changed. He was no longer dead in his trespasses and sins, but was alive and forgiven in Christ Jesus. As a Christian, he became a hard-charging, intelligent, hard-working, goal-focused, servant of Jesus. Paul's basic personality type was the same after his conversion as before his conversion, but after being saved he was totally changed in his orientation toward life.

Once we have identified our personality type, we have the wonderful privilege of yielding ourselves to God's Spirit so that we can be the best we can be. God's Spirit lives in all of His children, but the expression of the life of God in us will be seen through the creation gift of our basic personality. Proverbs 22:6 contains a truth that is often overlooked. "Train up a child in the way he should go. Even when he is old he will not depart from it." The phrase that we too quickly pass over is "way he should go" or "according to his own way or bent." This is a verse that is telling us something about what we might want to call personality type or temperament. Parents should treat all their children fairly but they cannot treat all their children the same because their children are not the same. They have basic personality differences. Children should not be forced to be just like each other. They should be taught the truth and expected to obey it. But, they should be brought up according to their own natural personality bent.

By knowing something about personality type in general we can learn to understand another person better. The key to using personality type in marriage is to identify who we are and who our mate is by using an instrument like the MBTI. The second step is to accept who we are and who our mate is. That is a difficult assignment and one that most married couples do not successfully accomplish. However, by accepting our personality type and the personality type of our mate, we can grow in intimacy as we build compatibility. The third step is to learn to appreciate the differences that exist between our personalities. The typical response to someone who is not like us is to conclude that one of us is wrong – usually the other person! If a person is guilty of violating Biblical teachings in their speech and conduct, they are wrong. But personality preference is more like trying to determine who is right among coffee drinkers: black, cream and sugar, cream with no sugar, sugar with no cream. There really is no right or wrong way to drink coffee. It all has to do with a person's taste preferences. Personality type does not deal with moral values but rather gives us observable behavior and relational traits. Learning to appreciate personality type differences between a husband and wife is virtually impossible for most couples without the power of the Holy Spirit working in them. God's promise is that we can do all things through Him who strengthens us (Philippians 4:13). We can learn to appreciate the differences in personality between us and our partner because God will give us the strength to do it.

If it is true that our personality type does not change over time, then we waste a lot of time and energy trying to change another person in that way. Some experts believe that most marital difficulties do not have solutions because they are rooted in personality differences that will not change. Learning to identify, accept, and appreciate our mate's personality can help us learn to adjust and adapt to the things that are different between us.

The big difference in introverts and extraverts that subtly creates division in the relationship is their source of motivational energy. Extraverts are empowered by the outside world. This external environment of people and interactions raises the level of their motivational strength. After being around people for some time, an extravert is even more outgoing. An introvert is quite different. They get their motivational energy from inside. Their inner world of thoughts and feelings gives them energy. To be around people for an extended period of time will drain an introvert's motivational strength.

At the end of the work day, an extraverted public relations man may come home to his introverted wife who has been working as a receptionist at a busy physician's office. She is spent because extraverted activity drains motivational energy from an introvert. The two are operating on two different levels of motivational strength. From this condition, false conclusions and judgments can be made. He may decide that she just doesn't care for him because she doesn't want to socialize, party, or gather with people and talk. She may conclude that he has lost interest in her because he never seems to want to spend a quiet evening alone with her. When a couple like this begins to see each other in light of each other's introverted or extraverted preference, they can make adjustments that will complement each other's personality gifts.

Extraverts like to think out loud. They would rather brainstorm with a few people than think something through alone. They have been known to change their opinion about something in the middle of a discussion. This "thinking out loud" can be seen by introverts as shallowness.

Introverts like to think things through. They may actually analyze something and come to a conclusion about it without even sharing their decision with anyone. You never get to fully know an introvert because they will not let you. Whatever you see or know about an introvert is usually representative of more that you do not know about them. An introvert's tendency to go within, withdraw, or just be quiet can be interpreted as aloofness or unfriendliness by an extravert.

An introvert-extravert couple may go to a party together. The introvert finds a nice place to sit, sip on some punch, and just observe what is going on around him while occasionally talking with one or two guys he knows. He is content and is actually having a good time until his extraverted wife notices him and thinks he needs someone to help him mix and mingle with people. When she pulls him away from his observation perch into the swarm of people, he stops having a good time.

The sensing-intuitive preference has to do with how we take in information about what is going on in the world around us. We all use our senses like taste, touch, feel, smell, see, etc. but an intuitive person will depend more heavily on something like a sixth sense. It has been described as a hunch or a feeling.

Sensors are more practical, realistic, detailed, and literal than intuitives who are more figurative, relational, and tend to think in terms of what is possible. Sensors are comfortable at managing what is, but intuitives are moved to create something new. Sensors can get lost in the nuts and bolts of a project while intuitives can see the big picture clearly but can almost completely miss what it will take to accomplish the project.

Sensors have a tendency to be observers of life who enjoy pleasure. Intuitives are people who have expectant attitudes and enjoy inspiration. An intuitive may want to achieve so intensely that they miss the joy of the present.

Sensors may enjoy living in the present so much that they fail to embrace the importance of entertainment or achievement.

Otto Kroeger and Janet M. Thuesen illustrate the differences in sensors and intuitives. "At an informal church service, an intuitive clergyman said, 'Let's sing two stanzas of hymn number 236." The hymn had five stanzas. A sensor from the congregation shouted out, 'Which two?' The intuitive pastor replied, 'Any two you want!'"[1]

An intuitive wife may want new and different romantic experiences while her sensing husband wants a romantic life that is practical and tied to the present. By learning to appreciate the differences, they can build a unique relationship that is both intimate and interesting.

The thinking-feeling function relates to how we make decisions. It is not a measure of intelligence or emotional health. Thinkers are more objective while feelers are more subjective. Feelers dislike conflict and work to have harmony. Thinkers want what is right according to their definition of right. Thinkers prefer facts to feelings while feelers desire affection, warmth, and sharing. Women more often have the feeling preference and men tend to prefer thinking. Thinkers prefer logic, reason and objective facts more than sentiment. They may suppress or ignore feelings that are not compatible with the facts. Feelers, on the other hand, value sentiment above logic and reason. They are more personable than thinkers and tend to be more tactful. They may ignore facts if that means feelings will be hurt. Feelers long to actually experience closeness and intimacy in marriage while thinkers are motivated to try and understand what intimacy means and how it works.

Thinkers are more likely to be people who value power whereas feelers are more likely to embrace empowerment. Thinkers may tend to control while feelers may tend to serve. Information is the essence of communication in a thinker's world. For a feeler sharing information is the beginning of an experience between people.

The final pair of preferences, judging and perceiving, have to do with our lifestyle in general. Judging does not mean judgmental but decisive. Judgers like structure and organization. They believe in the motto, "a place for everything and everything in its place." They are planners who bring order and deliberateness to their relationships. Perceivers, on the other hand, like to keep things open-ended and continue to collect information. While judgers may be too quick to make closure on something, perceivers have a tendency to leave things undecided too long. Judgers like a planned, orderly approach to just about everything. Perceivers are spontaneous and like to be more laid-back. They adjust well and do not need plans. They enjoy surprises and can even embrace change. Judgers believe in finishing what you start while perceivers believe in starting something new again and again. They do not put a priority on finishing something and may leave several things incomplete. Judgers like to have things settled. They are definite and purposeful. Perceivers are curious and tolerant. Judgers want to do things right. Perceivers want to experience all they can and miss nothing. Judgers believe in rules, schedules, policies, etc. Perceivers believe in spontaneity, freedom, and keeping their options open.

These two can actually work together quite well in marriage since the preferences describe lifestyle in general. Perceivers can help judgers relax while judgers can help perceivers become more organized.

We are wired differently. That is not a problem but can be a tremendous potential. Marriage is a relationship, a covenant, a partnership, a team of two, and an opportunity. Our personality type is one of the ingredients in how we build outstanding and fulfilling marriages. Our relationship to Christ is the power through which we can affirm how we are alike and appreciate how we are different. Personality is His creation gift to us.

Chapter 4

The Influence Of Birth Order

God is sovereign over everything and everybody. He is in control. He rules. This Biblical fact does not negate the freedom of people nor does it reduce our responsibility. Birth order is one of those areas that demonstrate God's sovereignty. We did not choose when we would be born or who our parents would be. Neither did we choose what size our family would be or where we would be in the birth order.

Throughout the years, people have observed that different birth orders have several common characteristics. Not everyone will have these specific traits but most people generally will follow the identifying marks of their birth order group. We are all products of the family in which we grew up. Even if that family was dysfunctional, blended, adopted, or in some way irregular, we still bear the mark of that group of people.

Many variables exist when we attempt to categorize birth order traits. If there have been five or more years between a person and their next sibling, the birth order traits are affected. It is almost like the birth order traits start over. When as many as 5 years or more are between siblings, both will likely have a mixture of traits. This unique combination will resemble their own natural birth order and also have many of the traits of an only child or a first born.

Other ways birth order traits are altered and become less predictable is when a child is adopted into a family or when a child in the family dies. The divorce and remarriage of parents, especially if blended families are involved, also influences birth order traits. The personalities of the parents or guardians affect birth order. Natural disasters can modify how birth order characteristics are clustered. Illness can also modify birth order traits. The death of a parent is a major disruption to the family system. There is also some evidence that indicates a child will take on some of the traits of the birth order of their same sex parent. It is possible that a last born son whose dad was a first born will have some last born traits in addition to the characteristics of a first born.

It is important to grasp that birth order is nothing more than a way of generally describing the group a person best fits. It is possible that a person could be last born, but because of different variables actually has traits that are more like a middle born or even a first born. The basic premise that seems to run consistently in birth order traits is that each child has a need to find their own place in the family. Children, more often than not, have a need for attention and will work to get that attention in one way or another. Kids will develop their identities by relating to other people in the family. They usually will take a place (develop a cluster of traits) that is not already possessed by a brother or sister.

Why is birth order significant in building a marriage that works? Because who we are and how we grew up will have some influence on who we are and how we relate when we are married. Merri Wallace in her book, <u>Birth Order Blues</u>, has noted, "As the child grows up, any unresolved jealousy, anger, insecurity, or resentment resulting from those early childhood experiences will shape her development, and be played out at school, at work, and in her adult relationships."[1]

Many psychiatrists, psychologists, and counselors over time have stressed the importance of birth order. Some think, next to our gender, it may be the single most influential factor in revealing how we relate to other people.

As a generalization, some research seems to indicate that last borns are often more popular with their peers and first borns and only children are less popular. As children are added to a family, the rules and discipline seem to become more relaxed and the structure not as strict. In most cases, first borns receive the most discipline and last borns the least amount of discipline.

Only children grow up in a predominantly adult world. They share the same traits as first borns but with added intensity. They typically are perfectionists who are driven to prove their worth and often live with self-imposed standards and expectations that are too high. As a result, only children can become discouraged people who battle feelings and thoughts of inferiority. Many are lonely because they grew up without brothers and/or sisters around. However, because of that, they usually develop discipline, creative imaginations and an ability to please the adults in their lives.

Only children and first born children have a tendency to be perfectionists and can be stubborn, opinionated, and unrelenting. Many are actually frustrated perfectionists and deal with discouragement on many different levels. They can be very critical and unforgiving. Since they are often very independent, they may find it difficult to ask for help. They can devote themselves strenuously to a task or work in order to prove their value and competence. Generally, they are goal-oriented, reliable, conscientious, well-organized, critical, scholarly, and serious-minded. They believe in rules and regulations and are usually loyal. As a rule, they want to be first and often become socially dominant. First born women, however, tend to deviate from this trait, and are more conforming than their male counterparts. All first borns and onlies believe strongly in law and order and are more naturally skilled in planning something than in spontaneously adapting to change. The only surprises they like are those that fit into their comfort zones.

First born and only children are achievers. Since they like things organized and structured, they may have little tolerance for a mate who is unorganized or too spontaneous. Many are scholarly types who can be tough minded. Some famous first born and only children are: Franklin Delano Roosevelt, Walter Cronkite, Bill Clinton, Winston Churchill, Joseph Stalin, Phyllis Schlafly, Mao Tse-tung, Albert Einstein, Galileo, Robespierre, Isaac Newton, Sigmund Freud, Oprah Winfrey, Clint Eastwood, James Earl Jones, and Peter Jennings.

Middle born people are the most difficult birth order to characterize. They are many times contradictions. A second born child is likely to be opposite of their older sibling, especially if they are of the same sex. Middle borns report that they sometimes felt like the odd person out in the family while growing up. They seemed to have some trouble finding their spot in the family constellation. This out of step or fifth wheel feeling often motivates them to concentrate on building friendships. They almost always have more friends than any of the other birth orders. Friends are important to them and they are heavily influenced by their friends. They can be rather free-spirited and good at the art of peacemaking. Tender-hearted, flexible, and team players are words that describe this birth order. They appear to be less fearful and driven than the first born but are also the most secretive and indecisive of all the birth orders. Because they are so eager and willing to compromise, they may stay in destructive relationships too long. When they are close in age to their older sibling, the two may be more competitive particularly if they are the same sex.

They can be overly cautious and downplay their own accomplishments. Some middle born people include: Harriet Beecher Stowe, Alfred Alder, Martin Luther King Jr., Anne Boleyn, David Letterman, Donald Trump, Fidel Castro, and George H. Bush.

Last borns love attention and often seek the spotlight in the family through entertaining, jokes, cuteness, helplessness or some other attention-getting strategy. They usually get more attention than anyone else in the family because everyone else in the family feels some degree of responsibility to care for the baby. They typically received the least amount of discipline from their parents (notably dads) and were put down more by their siblings. They may feel like they were not taken seriously when they were growing up. They tend to be people-oriented and are motivated to make a contribution to something constructive in life. They can develop the craft of manipulation and may also become excellent sales people. After a session of birth order during a marriage retreat, one of the participants approached the leader. He was the owner of a car dealership. "You know," he began. "I try to find out a person's birth order when they apply for a sales position. I have hired more last borns than any other birth order. They seem to make the best salespeople."

Some last borns will be undisciplined in their personal life and be consistently late for appointments, etc. They seem to be the least career-oriented of the birth orders and also the most light-hearted, particularly if they grew up in an intact and healthy family. However, most of them will have a drive to excel in some area of life. They are naturally good listeners

While growing up their problems are, as a rule, seen as trivial by their older siblings. As a result, they tend to embellish their experiences and become dramatic in their interpretations of their own difficulties. Many become artists. They normally do better in support roles than in positions of leadership. Insecurity and a lack of personal confidence can be issues for a number of last borns.

Some famous last borns are: Benjamin Franklin, Charles Darwin, John Calvin, John Knox, William Tyndale, Eddie Murphy, Steve Martin, Chevy Chase, and Catherine of Aragon, the first of Henry the VIII's six wives and the only one who was last born.

Twins present a different challenge to those who study birth order. In many cases, one twin will take on the characteristics of one birth order and the other twin will reflect traits of the next birth order. This is true particularly when the twins have been raised as individuals, dressed differently, had their own rooms, etc. Identical twins, unlike other brothers and sisters, find it hard to put distance between each other. They appear to be less willing to learn from older adults than other birth orders and are particularly talented at using their united power against their mother. Girl twins have the closest and longest lasting relationships with each other. Identical twin girls have the greatest struggle separating from each other. If twins have not established some degree of personal independence and individual identity by their college years, it may be difficult for them to marry.

Kevin Leman in <u>The New Birth Order Book</u> says, "No matter where twins may land in a family birth order, they wind up something of a first-born/second-born combination and are usually competitor and companion....but not always. Some twinships can turn into rivalries, particularly if the children are the same sex."[2]

People outside the immediate family relate to twins as though they were relating to one person. This can add to a twin's already strong sense of dependence on the other twin. They will develop different areas of individuality as they grow, but they will always have such a close tie to each other that marital intimacy may not sometimes measure up to the relationship they share together as twins. Twins can have great marriages, but they must be consciously aware of the deep connection they have with each other and not allow that closeness to hinder marital intimacy.

Birth order is something we cannot control but we can learn about ourselves by examining our place of birth in the family. Carl Whitaker once noted that there are really no individuals – only fragments of families. Growing up in a family is such a dynamic and unique experience that it shapes and influences our lives in significant and lasting ways.

Our place in our family of origin will lead to the accumulation of a cluster of behavioral traits. Those traits, when joined with other factors such as personality type and gender will contribute to our individuality. When we marry, those traits will sooner or later become apparent in our relationship.

Leman says, "For a happy marriage, find someone as opposite from your birth order as possible. Only children and last borns supposedly make the best match, followed by first borns and last borns. Next come the middle borns married to the last borns. Over the years as I have counseled thousands of couples, the most competitive, most volatile, and most discouraged are combinations where both spouses are first borns, or worse, both are only children."[3]

Birth order should not become the basis for marrying or not marrying someone just as personality type should not be the determining factor in selecting a mate. It is helpful to understand how birth order and personality type can impact our marriage. As a general rule we will have more challenges if we marry someone with the same birth order than someone who has a different birth order than us.

We occupy the particular birth order we have because of God's providential working. We can maximize our special birth order traits by realizing our position is not by chance or circumstance but by our Maker's design. By His grace we can accept our distinctiveness as a particular part of our family of origin, learn to change the negative qualities we are able to change, and have the wisdom to know the difference between the two. Birth order is not the last word on who we are destined to be. God is.

Chapter 5

Distinctively Male and Female

Genesis 1:27 says, "God created man in His own image, in the image of God He created him: male and female He created them."

Men and women are designed by God to be different. We are called to enjoy that difference in the relationship of marriage. But, too often our differences divide us instead of compelling us toward a greater intimacy. Enjoying the differences requires the grace of God and hard work. Differences in the marriage relationship are to be celebrated not attacked.

Someone has said, "A difference that makes no difference is no difference." Real and perpetual differences exist between men and women. These differences are one of the ways God has designed us. We are different physically, emotionally, and relationally. We see things differently and respond differently. We are even given different marital roles in Scripture. These differences allow us to build a special relationship together in which we complement each other and experience intimacy.

Men are called by God to be the spiritual leaders in the home. Both are called to obey God and be mutually submissive to each other as Christians. But the roles men and women have been assigned by God in marriage are different. According to Ephesians 5, men are to love their wives as Christ loved the Church and women are to be submissive to their husbands. The differences in men and women are reflected in the different roles God has given each.

A husband is to love his wife enough to die for her since that is exactly what Christ did for the Church. A wife is to submit to her husband as unto the Lord. She is to respond to his unconditional and sacrificial love for her by choosing to submit or rank under him in the administrative structure of the marriage. Both roles must be fully operational in order to build a more Godly and stronger marriage. Submission is a willing act of cooperation. Headship is a reflection of authority that assumes proper authority in the right spirit.

Larry Crabb has emphasized that headship is related to masculinity while femininity is related to submission. "A husband exercises headship over a wife when he expresses his manhood toward her…. Headship is not a badge to quickly grab when a decision must be made. It is a way of relating that reflects a husband's masculinity as he engages with his wife's femininity." He further relates that submission "consists of a woman's warmly receiving and meaningfully supporting a man's involvement in life in a way that encourages his godliness."[1]

John MacArthur believes that both nature and general custom reflect God's universal principle of man's role of authority and woman's role of subordination. I Corinthians 11:14-15 says, "Does not even nature itself teach you that if a man has long hair, it is a dishonor to him, but if a woman has long hair, it is a glory to her? For her hair is given to her for a covering." He states, "Men and women have distinctive physiologies. One obvious difference is the process of hair growth. Head hair develops in three stages: formation and growth, resting, and fallout. The male hormone testosterone speeds up the cycle so that men reach the third stage earlier than women. The female hormone estrogen causes the cycle to remain in stage one for a longer period, causing women's hair to grow longer than men's. Women are rarely bald because few ever reach stage three. This physiology is reflected in most cultures of the world when women wear their hair longer than men."[2] Roles and behavioral patterns throughout history have reflected the differences in men and women.

Men are more prone to give information or advice while women are more likely to give praise. Women are usually more verbal than men. This has been observed as early as four and five years by monitoring boys and girls at play on kindergarten playgrounds. Boys make noises like motors, growls, etc. Girls actually say words. It has been suggested that men have about 12,000 per day while women have about 24,000. By the end of the day, she still has about 10,000 words left for him while he has just about used up his quota!

Our brains are wired differently. Men are wired for doing, while women are wired for talking. Pierce J. Howard, in his book, The Owner's Manual For The Brain, has written that the "male differentiated brain finds it easier to handle multitasking, such as talking while building something. Talking, which uses the left hemisphere, doesn't interfere in a major way with building, which is visual-spatial and uses the right hemisphere. Because the female-differentiated brain handles visual-spatial tasks in both hemispheres, building and talking, which both use the left hemisphere, interfere with each other." Because a woman has a corpus callosum (which connects the two hemispheres) that is up to 23 percent thicker than a man, she is able to have greater access to both her own feelings and the feelings of others as she produces her language. Howard continues, "The male's separation of language specialization in the left hemisphere and emotional specialization in the right helps to explain his traditional ineptness at connections with his language production via his thinner corpus callosum."[3]

Many people believe that men listen to women less than women listen to men, but there appears to be some evidence that men actually hear what women are saying but they do not connect with them. Women do seem to enjoy sharing the details of their lives more than men do. Women are often looking for a connection and not a solution to their difficulty. Men often feel pressure to provide a solution or to fix her problem. For example, Judy comes home from work where she has had an unusually bad day. She was treated unjustly by her supervisor and felt like she was being harassed. When she comes home, after a few minutes of transition, she begins to tell her husband Mark about all the details. Mark begins to feel stressed. He looks at his watch and figures it will take Judy at least an hour to share all this. He is angered that she was treated badly and wants to do something about it. He volunteers to break her boss's nose, but that is met with absolute rejection by Judy. There is a game on TV that he must see. Dinner is still ahead. He quickly surmises that this sharing time by Judy will mess up his plans. He also feels his own blood pressure rising over the way his wife was treated. He concludes that he must fix this soon. He begins to listen intently and interrupts often to be sure he understands the situation. He moves her to a summary and then he makes the fatal pronouncement, "Ok, Judy, I think I understand." Then he lists what she has shared. She agrees he has it right so far. He then says, "This is what you need to do…" After citing a plan of action for her when she returns to her job the next day, he says to himself, "Problem solved. Crisis averted. I fixed it!" What he doesn't realize is that he fixed nothing. In fact, Judy was not even looking for a solution, she was looking for a connection with him and he missed it.

If men can recognize that they do not generally make connections with their wives as well as they think they do, they would then be able to develop the skills that would allow them to make better connections. Wives can also help make better connections with their husbands by editing their speeches to a shorter and more concise form.

Women handle emotional issues better than men with less wear and tear on their bodies. Men are more likely to repress, avoid, or deny feelings. Women, on the other hand, seem to be much better at sharing their feelings. Men have feelings but those feelings are almost always accessed through a more analytical rather than emotional process. When men are aroused emotionally, they want to do something. When women are aroused emotionally, they want to talk. The traits that typically characterize the male brain include aggression, competition, self-assertion, self-confidence, and self-reliance. Men usually are better at math while women do better with language, memory, social awareness, and building relationships.

Men may actually reveal how they are feeling through sharing a story. They may have difficulty formulating their feelings in words, but they can identify with the emotions in a story, movie, etc. Have you ever noticed how much men swap stories and how seldom women do? Men are more analytical and less expressive emotionally not because they don't have feelings but because they are not as good at expressing those feelings as women. They also tend to be more indirect than women whey they do express their feelings. Men usually see home as a place to relax whereas women see home as a place where good communication should take place.

Because women have a greater capacity for dealing with emotions and since they are more gifted at nurturing, this is an area where a woman can encourage and empower her husband in his journey. Mutual sharing of feelings can be very healthy, but it must be done in an atmosphere where there is mutual respect, support, understanding and encouragement. Men and women share how they feel differently. Neither one is wrong. They are just different. Men need to be willing to listen and process their feelings while they are doing something while women need to be willing to move beyond just talking to doing something. Both can moderate how they deal with emotional issues so that both can feel more confident in dealing with the other. An old slogan about marriage is worth repeating here, "Each for the other and both for the Lord."

Men are usually more competitive than women whereas women are more likely to yearn for companionship with their husbands. In their conversations, women may say something like "yeah" or "I understand." What men hear is "I agree." That is not what women mean.

Men think about sex several times a day while a married woman may think about sex about twice a week. Some men may have 20 to 30 times more testosterone in their bodies than women. Testosterone is a hormone that promotes sexual drive, aggression, and competition. Testosterone varies with men, but testosterone is higher in the morning for both men and women, yet most sexual activity between husbands and wives occurs at night.

Testosterone increases after men go through a vigorous exercise time or following a competitive sport in which they won the contest. Lower testosterone levels do not mean weakness in a man. It does take away extreme aggression and the combative attitude that characterizes high testosterone people.

Women have a higher immunity for fighting viruses than men. They also have a much higher level of estrogen than men. This hormone influences things like caring, nurturing, etc. Women have more migraine headaches than men. They have a higher incidence of depression and their hearts are two thirds smaller than a man's. They live about seven years longer than a man and regain consciousness more quickly after anesthesia. While aspirin reduces a man's risk of stroke, it does not lessen the risk for a woman.

A man wants to feel like he is needed by his wife. To feel unneeded is a huge setback for a man. A woman likes to feel like she is cherished and needs to see affection from her husband. Wives' chief complaint about their husbands is that they do not listen, do not talk to them, or are distracted with other things. She often feels like she is playing second fiddle to something or someone else in life. Husbands typically complain that they feel like their wives are always trying to change them or that the wives talk too much.

John Gray in the popular book, <u>Men Are From Mars, Women are From Venus</u> writes, "Men and women generally are unaware that they have different emotional needs." He then cites the primary relational needs of a woman: caring, understanding, respect, devotion, validation, and reassurance. The needs of a man are: trust, acceptance, appreciation, admiration, approval, and encouragement.[4]

Willard F. Harley in his book, <u>His Needs, Her Needs</u>, said, "The typical wife doesn't understand her husband's deep need for sex any more than the typical husband understands his wife's deep need for affection." He listed the most basic needs of married couples: For men it is: sexual fulfillment, recreational companionship, an attractive spouse, domestic support, and admiration. For women it is: affection, conversation, honesty and openness, financial support, and family commitment.[5]

Healthy self-esteem is important for anyone. But how do we get it? For wives, their self-esteem has traditionally been tied to their husbands. For husbands, their self-esteem has been tied to their work. However, both of these sources of self-esteem are flawed. You could lose your husband and you could lose your job. What would happen to your self esteem? There is a better way. Romans 8:1 says, "Therefore there is now no condemnation for those who are in Christ Jesus." A Christian is justified by faith in Jesus Christ (Rom. 5:2). This is a legal declaration by God that we are perfect in Christ. We are not perfect in practice, but we are perfect in our position (in Christ) before God. God loves, accepts, and forgives the believer. That is a position of value and worth. It is based on God's grace. We are that way, regardless of what happens to us. This position is the best foundation for building an attitude that has strong self-esteem. It works equally well for men and women. It is a self-esteem not based on people or jobs but on the faithfulness of God Himself. When we can take that thought and apply it in the arena of our relationships, we will have a stronger confidence and a deeper personal worth that will in turn empower us to work on building a better marriage.

Deborah Tannen in her work, <u>You Just Don't Understand</u>, has written, "To most women, conflict is a threat to connection, to be avoided at all costs. Disputes are preferably settled without direct confrontation. But to many men, conflict is the necessary means to which status is negotiated... It is not that women do not want to get their way, but that they do not want to purchase it at the cost of conflict."[6] Men seem to know this and can often exploit their wives. Probably the most expressive emotion in men is anger. They don't mind conflict because of their competitive drive to win. However, men are often very reluctant to share other feelings with their wives because they feel threatened, vulnerable, and weak. The real weakness, of course, is in not sharing. The truth is that anytime we can face our feelings and put them in the stream of our consciousness we will eventually gain more control over them. When we push those feelings down inside through repression and denial, they have more control over us. The key seems to be that both men and women recognize the traits of each other and make it as comfortable as possible for the other to share the true feelings of their heart.

The differences that exist among men and women are also enormous. Many different elements converge in our lives that help to create the differences between us. Every marriage must be customized to meet the challenges of knowing and learning to enjoy the differences. Sometimes we can change but at all times we must be willing to accept our mates for who they are. By accepting our mate, we are more likely to see positive changes in our mate.

God has created us to be different, and He has redeemed us to be different. As Christians He has called us to live out roles in marriage that both reflect the differences that naturally exist between us and honor Him as we do it. Differences should not divide us, but enable us to build something together we could never build alone. Women are naturally more nurturing while men are naturally more competitive. Wives are empowered to fulfill their greatest potential in the marriage through the disposition of a healthy submissiveness. Men are given the ability to reach their potential as a doer through the attitude and practice of a loving headship. The motive for both husband and wife is the glory of God and the good of the marriage. When that is the motive, and His Word is obeyed, the results will be evident.

Chapter 6

The Friendship Factor

Next to faith in Christ, the friendship of a husband and wife may be the single most important factor in determining the longevity of a marriage.

In his book, <u>The Seven Principles For Making Marriage Work</u>, John Gottman has noted that it takes courage, determination, and resiliency to maintain a long-lasting relationship. He writes, "The determining factor in whether wives feel satisfied with the sex, romance, and passion in their marriage is, by 70 percent, the quality of the couple's friendship. For men, the determining factor is, by 70 percent, the quality of the couple's friendship. So men and women come from the same planet after all."[1]

Couples, who work at building and maintaining their friendship, create such strong and consistently positive thoughts and exchanges that negative feelings are usually overcome without major upset. For married couples, friendship feeds romance. The Old Testament book, Song of Solomon, is about romantic love. In chapter two of that book, the king's wife speaks of her lover, "This is my beloved and this is my friend" (vs. 16). Two critical aspects of a rewarding romantic life are fondness and admiration.

In the marital relationship when the number of positive exchanges and pleasing behaviors goes up, the marriage is more compatible. Because it is more compatible, it is more satisfying and rewarding for both parties. For friendship to grow and develop, positive and pleasing behaviors between husband and wife are essential.

A friend is a companion and a confidant. A friend is someone you know, like, and trust. Negative encounters with each other lead to the demise of a marriage while positive interactions promote both enthusiasm and good will.

We live in a culture that is negative. Some estimate that as much as 90 percent of everything that comes into our lives is negative. We also know that it takes about 10 positive strokes just to neutralize one negative. What chance do we have of living positive lives? The answer revolves around what feeds our lives. If we are plugged into something that constantly feeds us positive energy, we can live positive lives. We will not find that source in the world, but we do discover it is the product of God's Spirit in the lives of His people. Galatians 5:22-23 tells us that the "fruit of the Spirit is love, joy, peace, patience, kindness, goodness, faithfulness, gentleness, self-control; against such things there is no law." This list is not exhaustive but representative of the positive attributes the Spirit of God produces in the lives of God's children when they are filled with His Spirit. Christians who are committed to know God and His Word and then live out those principles in their marriages will find more than enough positive power to create pleasing exchanges between each other.

I Corinthians 7:32-34 says, "I want you to be free from concern. One who is unmarried is concerned about the things of the Lord, how he may please the Lord; but the one who is married is concerned about the things of the world, how he may please his wife, and his interests are divided. The woman who is unmarried, and the virgin, is concerned about the things of the Lord, that she may be holy both in body and spirit; but one who is married is concerned about the things of the world, how she may please her husband." In this passage of Scripture is a tremendous insight for building a positive relationship and strong compatibility: the please principle! Paul is not attempting to destroy marriage or persuade people from getting marriage. He is simply stating a basic fact. If a person has the gift of celibacy, he or she can best serve God with all their time, talent, and energy. They can devote their lives 100 percent to the work of God. However, if a person is married, they must devote some of their time to the marriage. Since marriage is ordained by God, it certainly is not wrong to build a good marriage. Marriage is an earthly relationship. In heaven there is no marriage. But here on earth, marriage becomes an illustration of the relationship Christ has with His bride the church. So if a person is married they, by nature of the relationship, must seek to please God and please their mate. Their interests are divided so to speak. Here's the key Paul is sharing with us. If you have a wife, please her. If you have a husband, please him.

The principle of pleasing must follow the constraints of common sense and moral integrity. An unhealthy dependency is not a viable option for building an intimate and good relationship. Suppose your wife tells you that it would please her if you went down to the local bank and robbed it. A clear teaching of Scripture would be violated if you stole money. We should not disobey God in order to please our mate, but within the boundaries of Scriptural liberty, we should strive to please him or her.

The word "please" in I Corinthians 7 is the Greek word "aresko." It is used 17 times in the New Testament with 14 of those occurring in the writings of Paul. Originally it meant to reconcile or make peace with someone. In general it means a definite attitude that seeks to care for, gratify, satisfy, entertain, or provide pleasure for someone.

When a husband and wife are both committed to pleasing each other, compatibility in that marriage is bound to grow. Compatibility is not being alike but knowing what pleases your mate and doing it. It is the ability to live together in harmony. One of the chief reasons often cited for why marriages fail is a lack of pleasing behaviors. We know that happy couples exchange more positive and fewer negative behaviors than unhappy couples. The more the number of pleasing exchanges increases in a marriage the greater the level of overall satisfaction in the marriage.

We all experience some negativity in marriage. What is a healthy ratio of positive to negative exchanges? Estimates range from a low of five to a high of twenty positives. The consensus is that five positives for every one negative is the threshold. If a couple has 17% or higher negative exchanges, improvement is needed in order to build a more vibrant compatibility. The more positives and fewer negatives we can realize, the better.

Albert Einstein and his wife were happily married for over 60 years. He developed his own theory of the number of positive to negative exchanges needed for a good marriage. He once noted, "One incorrect input requires eleven correct inputs to make things right."

Pleasing can be understood as making deposits into the heart bank of our mate. The currency we use comes in various denominations such as accommodating, complimenting, helping, satisfying, encouraging, giving, and understanding. Pleasing involves spending time together and growing in our respect and care for each other.

God designed marriage and called husbands and wives to please each other as they live together in this one-flesh relationship. Husbands and wives are supposed to be friends... best friends. In Genesis, for the first time we read something that was not good. Genesis 2:18 says, "Then the Lord God said, 'It is not good for the man to be alone; I will make him a helper suitable for him.'" Eve was suitable for Adam and Adam was suitable for Eve. The potential for compatibility resides in each man and woman who follows God's truth in relating to the other person. Suitable means in "front of, in sight of, before." The idea is to be conspicuous before the other person and not secretive. Suitable is that which corresponds to the other person. Adam and Eve were definitely made for each other! They were soul mates. Eve was like him, but also different from him. Man and woman are suitable for each other in marriage. No other combination is right in God's sight. We correspond to each other. We can experience the compatibility we need in order to experience the joys of married life. The fuel that drives the engine of compatibility is knowing what pleases your mate and doing it.

Adam and Eve were created for each other. The fall of man into sin corrupted every relationship including marriage. Today, we need to be more than sons and daughters of Adam and Eve; we must be sons and daughters of God through the new birth in Christ Jesus. Our capacity to enjoy marriage, honor God, and be a blessing to others is directly related to the quality of our relationship with God Himself.

Building compatibility is a process in which we make progress. However, there is a strange sort of phenomenon that appears to happen when a couple goes through the dating and/or courtship time of their relationship. They do so many pleasing things for each other. They often sacrifice and do things with an unconditional type of giving. They are focused on doing everything they can to make the other person happy and they try to avoid anything that would displease them. However, when the realities of married life begin to sink in, they often change their strategy. It seems they revert back to a more selfish way of living where they seek to do everything they can to please themselves and avoid doing anything to make themselves unhappy.

While we are courting, it is relatively easy to be other-focused. After all, we really do not know the other person that well. But, after we are married and get to know them better and better, we tend to become more self-centered. This is a typical and serious problem in marriages. We please them the most when we know them the least and too often please our mates the least when we know them the best. This should not be. What is behind it? Why do we change from being other-focused to being more self-centered? Perhaps one of the reasons is that the chase is over and we have won the prize. However, a more subtle danger is more likely. We begin to walk in pride. As Christians we are instructed to walk by faith but when we fail to maintain our daily walk with Christ, we are already walking in pride. When that happens, relationships will invariably be affected.

Hebrews 12:2 reminds us to "lay aside every encumbrance and the sin which so easily entangles us, and let us run with endurance the race that is set before us." What is the sin that so easily entangles us? The sin theologically is unbelief. Psychologically, it is pride. Unbelief and pride are like two sides of the same coin. Pride comes before the fall. Pride will bring us low, but humility will lead us to blessing. Self-centered mates live in pride and it has many side affects – none of them positive.

Gottman has identified what he calls "The Four Horsemen of The Apocalypse."[2] These are four disastrous ways of relating to each other in marriage. They are likely all expressions of a prideful state of heart. If all four of these practices are occurring simultaneously and being practiced habitually, the marriage is failing and on the road to destruction. In order of importance they are:

1- <u>Criticism</u> is when a mate is consistently being attacked. It is more than just a specific behavior but is the ongoing activity of accusing and blaming the other person. A complaint is specific but criticism is general. A complaint can be good because it focuses on something. But criticism is not good because it condemns someone.

2- <u>Contempt</u> involves the intention to insult or injure your mate psychologically. Negative thoughts are verbalized through name-calling, hostile humor, mocking, ridicule, and body language like rolling your eyes, etc.

3- <u>Defensiveness</u> seeks to retaliate against your mate while defending yourself. It is a way of exhibiting your own feeling of superiority. Defensive actions include denying responsibility, making excuses, making negative assumptions about your mate, and cross-complaining.

4- <u>Stonewalling</u> is primarily done by men (about 85 percent of the time). It is the most negative and powerful of the four and sends a message of disapproval by creating emotional distance. It can be described as withdrawing, disengaging, or shutting down.

When all four of these "horsemen" line up in a consistent pattern, the marriage is in deep trouble. When these four destructive forces unite, the couple has become more like enemies than friends. The plunge into ruin can be turned around if both husband and wife are committed to making a new start and focusing less on self and more on the mate. Compromise at this stage becomes a viable instrument for healing but the greatest hope lies in a devoted commitment to Christ. We are 100 percent responsible for our souls. We are 50 percent responsible for our marriage. That doesn't mean we should ever give less than 100 percent but sometimes a marriage fails because two people are not together giving their all to the relationship.

Healing can come to a marriage from God. When and if it does, you can be sure the development of friendship will be a clear sign of a marriage that is not only on the road to healing but on the road to health as well.

Even friends disagree. Disagreements are not the determining factor in the health of a marriage. The content of our disagreement is not usually the most important contributor to marital discord. The most significant thing is how we argue. It is possible to disagree with a person's ideas, opinions, actions, and still affirm the person as a friend. This is the quality of marital life that resonates with strength.

Positive and pleasing exchanges make a huge difference in a marriage. Without them we can be legally married, but with them we can have a flourishing and fulfilling relationship. A good exercise for you would be to make a list of all the things you know that please your mate and then ask him or her to do the same. Then make a list of what pleases you. Ask your mate to do the same. Combine the lists and come up with an edited version. Then put into practice the things you now know please your mate.

Proverbs 17:17 says a "friend loves at all times." In order to create a stable and fulfilling marriage, husbands and wives must be growing in their friendship with each other. When couples care for each other, confidence and good feelings tend to increase while frustration and anger tends to decrease. Friendship means caring and God certainly desires for His people to care for each other in marriage.

Chapter 7

The Sexual Key

Sex is one of the most powerful, perverted, and misunderstood forces on the face of the earth! If sex and sexual innuendos were removed from all advertising, we would not recognize the ads we saw. We are sexual people and this God-given gift has been used, misused, and abused. There are some essential things we must know about sex, but that information must be understood in the right context.

Men and women are capable of sexual pleasure. Both men and women have sex drives and are capable of orgasms. We have sexual organs that allow us to enjoy pleasure and also reproduce children. Sex is good, but it can be bad even when it is not sinful. Christians in this century can enjoy a healthy sexuality, or they can endure unfulfilling sexual relations in marriage.

The only right moral context for sex is marriage. The control and enjoyment of sex is God's design for us and that balance is achieved only in the marriage relationship. Even though the culture at large embraces all kinds of sexual experiences and has little respect for the institution of marriage, the truth about sex remains unchanged. Hebrews 13:4 says, "Marriage is to be held in honor among all, and the marriage bed is to be undefiled; for fornicators and adulterers God will judge." That is a stern warning that underscores the sanctity of marriage. Sex outside of marriage is sex out of control and out of bounds morally. Sex inside the covenant of marriage is something that can bring great pleasure and personal closeness.

While everyone has sexual capabilities, not everyone experiences the same degree of satisfaction with sex. All people do not have the same intensity level in their sex drive. Men typically have stronger sexual drives than women and are more focused on the physical. Women may have strong sex drives (even stronger than some men) but it is usually connected with the warmth and quality of the relationship more than the sheer physical pleasure involved. Both men and women are capable of possessing strong sex drives. Men are more dependent on direct genital stimulation and are aroused by the visual, while women are more attracted to caring, touching, snuggling, and the emotional intimacy that comes from being in a close relationship.

Testosterone is a major hormone supplying much of the power in a man's sex drive. The sex drive itself is located in the brain. Archibald Hart in his book, Healing

Life's Addictions, has written, "The human sexual drive operates out of the cortex, that thin outer layer of the brain where all learning takes place. The fact that our sex drive is controlled by our brains also means that we can take our sex drive and add power to it with thoughts, fantasies, and preferences. The more we enhance our sex drive this way, the more addictive it becomes."[1]   For both men and women, our sexual appetite is a product of the brain. It is more about how we think than anything else. How we have been trained or conditioned to think about sex becomes a major factor in determining the kind of sexual relationship we will experience inside of marriage. For many of us, we must often go through the difficult task of relearning what we improperly learned or thought earlier about sex. The good news is that we can repair bad habits and replace them with healthy and Godly patterns of thought.

The difference in male and female sexuality has been described as the difference between the tortoise and the hare.   Men are aroused quickly and generally experience an orgasm sooner than women.   Women are aroused slower. They are capable of multiple orgasms even though most women do not experience this.   Women usually report that they enjoy a slower route to sexual release than men do. It is estimated that about 10% of women never experience an orgasm and about 25 percent of women have some type of orgasm difficulties some of the time. Men are driven to achieve an orgasm while women are more driven to enjoy the act of lovemaking itself. Men often feel frustrated when they do not experience orgasm while women often report that the physical closeness and hugging can satisfy them. The National Study on the Sexuality of Christian Women interviewed over 2,000 Christian women and discovered how much women value relational closeness with their husbands. "The women in our study overwhelmingly wanted closeness. When asked what they like most about having sex, 90 percent chose physical closeness and/or emotional closeness."[2]

Creativity can be a boost to a couple's sexual enthusiasm and excitement. One husband decided he would rent a Superman costume. He, with his wife's permission, tied her wrists and ankles to the bed posts. As she lay there naked, he jumped out of the bathroom in his Superman costume. He leaped up from the foot of the bed intending to land on the bed. However, when he jumped up, he hit his head on a paddle fan that was running overhead. That knocked him off balance. He then hit his head on the foot of the bed and hit it again on the hardwood floor as he fell with a thud. There was an eerie silence in the room. His wife called his name. Nothing. She got louder. Nothing. She finally began to shout "Help!" Their next door neighbor was outside and heard her screams. The front door was unlocked so he followed the screams to the bedroom. He opened the door and saw his neighbor's wife tied to the bed and immediately shut the door and called 911. As it turns out the husband had a mild concussion and had been temporarily knocked unconscious. It was an embarrassing time for them both.

Psalm 139:14 declares, "I will give thanks to You; for I am fearfully and wonderfully made." God designed our bodies. Sex has the potential to be satisfying and pleasurable for both men and women. A woman's clitoris has only one purpose: pleasure. The clitoris is a small round organ that is made up of erectile tissue. It is similar to a man's penis. In their book, <u>Sex Matters To Women</u>, Sallie Foley, Sally Kope, and Dennis Sugrue note, "The visible part of the clitoris has thickly clustered nerve endings, even more than the head of a penis, making it an organ often described as exquisitely sensitive."[3] About 30 percent of women report that they always experience an orgasm. However, most of these women probably experience orgasm during intercourse because of the direct clitoral stimulation before intercourse began. In fact, Hart, Weber, and Taylor report that about 2/3 of women cannot reach orgasm through intercourse alone.

The please principle found in I Corinthians 7 should also be practiced in the marriage bed. Orgasm does not happen in the clitoris but it is the trigger that contributes greatly to the sensate and pleasurable feeling of orgasm. Most women probably need around 15 minutes of direct clitoral stimulation in order to reach orgasm. The sexual intimacy we should enjoy in marriage involves husband and wife pleasing each other by giving each other pleasure. In I Corinthians 7:3-5, Paul writes, "The husband must fulfill his duty to his wife, and likewise also the wife to her husband. The wife does not have authority over her own body, but the husband does; and likewise also the husband does not have authority over his own body, but the wife does. Stop depriving one another, except by agreement for a time, so that you may devote yourselves to prayer, and come together again so that Satan will not tempt you because of your lack of self-control."

Another sexually sensitive part of a woman's genitalia has been referred to as the "G" spot. Named after a German gynecologist, Ernst Grafenberg, who described an area within the vagina on the upper wall, between the opening and the cervix, this spot enlarges when stimulated and can result in orgasm for women. Foley, Kope, and Sugrue state, "It should be kept in mind that because more than one nerve group can be stimulated at the same time, simultaneous G spot stimulation and clitoral stimulation are mutually enhancing. Although direct stimulation of the cervix or feelings stretched by penile girth can be pleasurable for some women, the major source of genital response is stimulation of the clitoris and nerve endings within the first two to three inches of the vagina. These highly erogenous areas, including the G spot, are well within the reach of even an unusually small penis."[4]

In men the testosterone level has a direct influence on their ability to pick up sexual cues from their wives and respond physically. The lower the testosterone, the more likely the man will miss his mate's signal. As men age, the level of testosterone in their bodies decreases resulting in fewer spontaneous thoughts about sex. As long as a man stays healthy, his interest in sex will still be strong but he will not be as obsessive about it as he was earlier in life.

Both men and women experience fluctuations in their sex drives. Some contributors to this fluctuation include hormonal levels, emotional condition, physical health, level of energy, and outward circumstances.

Historically, people have thought of sexual intimacy as involving three stages: desire, arousal, and orgasm. Some have criticized this model because it seems to describe the process of a man rather than a woman. Even prior to the arousal stage, a man should romance his wife for hours prior to the time of sex. When they come together for sex, the pre-season should last about 30 minutes (hugging, caressing, kissing, direct clitoral stimulation, and other mutually pleasing and erotic exchanges involved in foreplay). The season is the time of actual sexual intercourse. Most men overestimate this time. The average couple will spend between three and 10 minutes in sexual intercourse. The post-season is the time for snuggling and cuddling. This is often the most intimate time for a woman. The two may drift off to sleep in this position or just rest in each other's embrace. It should last 30 minutes or longer. The idea of a "quickie" that is promoted so often in the media is not realistic. In fact, the time of lovemaking should take about an hour or longer.

Some elements that can hinder good sexual relations include negative feelings toward your mate, poor communication, lack of trust, anxiety about how you look, lack of sensitivity, and too many distractions or interruptions. The atmosphere should be private and comfortable. One young couple put their young son in his bed for a nap on a Sunday afternoon. They went to their bedroom and began to engage in sex. The man looked up from under the covers and saw his young son standing right beside the bed! He popped back under the covers. His wife got up and took the boy back to his room. The son kept asking his mom what the two of them were doing. She replied, "You know how you like to watch wrestling on TV? Well, daddy and I like to wrestle. It's fun." This inquisitive youngster wouldn't stop, "But why were you naked?" She thought quick on her feet and said, "Oh, that's just the way daddy and I like to wrestle." He seemed to be satisfied with that explanation. A couple of weeks later, the family had gathered at her parent's home for an extended family meal. At the crowded lunch table, the little boy announced, "Granddad, did you know that mama and daddy like to get naked and wrestle in the bed!" The mom wanted to crawl under the table. The environment for a married couple engaging in sex should be private. It may also be a good idea to lock the bedroom door!

A good adage for most of us would be to look as good as we can, be as healthy as we can, and smell as good as we can. The time worn statement, "Cleanliness is next to Godliness" is especially applicable to sexual intimacy.

In the Song of Solomon some beautiful and discreet sexual language is used as the king and his wife engage in sexual romance. In chapter seven Solomon speaks to his lover, "Your stature is like a palm tree, and your breasts are like its clusters. I said, 'I will climb the palm tree, I will take hold of its fruit stalks.' Oh, may your breasts be like clusters of the vine, and the fragrance of your breathe like apples, and your mouth like the best wine!" (vs. 6-9a). A person would shimmy up a palm tree with arms and legs wrapped around the trunk of the tree. It was hard work! But, the sweet taste of the fruit was worth it. Solomon compares his wife's breasts with clusters of the vine. He is describing a sensation that is sweet and pleasurable. He longs to kiss and caress his wife. He desires to enjoy sex with her. Song of Solomon 8:3 depicts sexual foreplay. It is not a statement about sexual position, but it is a picture of sexual posture. "Let his left hand be under my head and his right hand embrace me." With his right hand he touches her genitalia and breasts. It is a portrait of sexual love in marriage.

She responds to him in 7:9b-12, "It goes down smoothly for my beloved, flowing gently through the lips of those who fall asleep. I am my beloved's and his desire is for me. Come, my beloved, let us go out into the country, let us spend the night in the villages. Let us rise early and go to the vineyards; Let us see whether the vine has budded and its blossoms have opened, and whether the pomegranates have bloomed. There I will give you my love." She is looking for a place of solitude for herself and her husband. She wants privacy and romance. Her desire is to give Solomon erotic love and she ties it strongly to the relationship with him. She likes his body, but she is more excited by him. Together, they give themselves for the sexual pleasure of the other. In turn, they are also pleased.

There is a big difference between having sex and actually making love. The Song Of Solomon presents in tasteful and elegant language, a husband and wife making love. Sex between husband and wife is intended for pleasure. It is spiritual at its core. We are to honor God with our bodies and be faithful and loyal to our spouses for life.

Chapter 8

The Power Of Good Communication

Someone has quipped that the greatest misunderstanding about communication is the idea that we have actually done it! Communication, like maturity, is more of a process instead of a state. Good communication is dynamic and alive rather than fixed and static.

Many people have taken courses or training in grammar, writing, or speaking. However, very few people have ever received any training in how to listen. That is compelling because listening is over half of effective communication. How a message is received is more important than how it is sent. Both are essential, but listening is more critical than we ever imagined. The majority of us think erroneously of communication as talking.

Linear communication is one-way. It is sending a message without any dialogue or feedback. It can be dangerous and will be distorted after it has passed through about three different people. Circular communication is what we must work on if we want to build a strong, healthy and intimate marriage. Circular communication involves asking questions and clarifying meanings. It avoids assuming we know what the other means and risks asking simple questions in order to be sure we know what they mean.

Our circulatory system pumps over 1,800 gallons of blood through 62,000 miles of blood vessels daily. As long as there are no blockages, we generally are healthy, but if there is an obstruction, we are physically in trouble. Circular communication is like that. A blockage in our marital communication system is a problem that can lead to a breakdown of the relationship.

Interpersonal communication can be understood by recognizing its three vital components. In relationships, our words constitute seven percent; the way we share those words, 38 percent; and the nonverbal or body language makes up 55 percent. How we send a message is more critical than the message we send. Our words can be clear but our actions (facial expression, hand movements, body position, tone of voice, etc) can send a totally different and even contradictory message.

Basically, over 90 percent of the impression we make on another person is found in how we look and sound. People are more likely to carry away an impression than they are information, particularly in relationships.

Really experiencing the personal connectedness that effective communication brings is an encounter with intimacy itself. However, miscommunication is more often experienced in marriage than communication. James Dobson has emphasized that all miscommunication results from differing assumptions. Luke 2:41-45 illustrates this point. Jesus had gone up with Mary and Joseph to the Passover Week Observance. This was a huge social gathering in addition to being a religious festival. Traveling in those days was considerably different than today. The women, probably with some male escorts for protection, would leave earlier than the men. The men would leave about noon and catch up with the women about sunset. The Bible records that when Mary and Joseph were reunited in the caravan that was traveling back to Nazareth, they realized they had left Jesus in Jerusalem. Why? How could such a thing happen? This was no ordinary child and they knew it. What might have happened is that Mary looked for Jesus before she left Jerusalem with the women and assumed he must be with Joseph. Joseph likely did the same thing and assumed Jesus was with Mary. When they met, they realized their assumptions had led to a big problem. They spent the night, took another day to travel back to Jerusalem, and found Jesus in the Temple area on the third day.

Assumptions can be very dangerous things in communication. In order to connect intimately with our mates, we must avoid them. Active and emphatic listening is a powerful tool we can consistently use to aid in eliminating poor communication. Listening is not easy. In fact, it is hard work. Most of us appear to have the habit of listening to our mate until we disagree with them. Then we stop listening and start preparing our defense. The purpose of listening is not to agree but to understand. I Peter 3:7 speaks to husbands, "...live with your wives in an understanding way..." A husband cannot understand his wife unless he learns to listen to her. When a person feels like they have been understood, you can disagree with them in a much healthier and less divisive manner.

Another common difficulty in marriages is related to differing expectations. Most people get married with some type of mental image or expectations about what their marriage ought to be. The problem is that these expectations are seldom shared. Sometimes they are not shared because they are simply too high. The expectations couples have in their hearts must be shared with each other. Only then, can needless misunderstanding be avoided and good adjustments be made.

One proven technique for developing better listening skills is to practice the acrostic SOLER.

S – Face the other person squarely.

O – Have an open posture. Do not cross your arms, legs, wrists, ankles, etc.

L- Lean slightly forward. This will help you be more attentive and will also send a message to the other person that you are interested in what they are sharing.

E- Maintain eye contact.

R- Relax!

If you practice this little formula as you listen, you will probably discover an increase in your personal listening ability and a greater degree of effectiveness in your marital communication. The majority of us overestimate our ability to listen well. Most of us think we remember around 80 percent of what we hear when in actuality we only remember approximately 25 percent. Hearing is natural, but listening is a skill we learn and develop over our lifetime.

Everyone wants to be understood. That means they must, at least, be heard. Everyone has a story to tell but not everyone has someone who wants to hear it. In order to mature in intimacy, a couple must continue to work on the art of listening. That will involve putting our self-focus aside, working hard to identify exactly what feelings and thoughts our partner is sharing, and making statements and asking questions that lead to a better understanding of our partner's feelings and thoughts. Misunderstanding and wrong conclusions are easily seen when we fail to listen. Some personalities are naturally more prone to speak up than others. In fact a sensing, thinking, judging personality type may think they know the answer before there is a question. For someone to interrupt their mate before they have shared fully their message is not only rude but unintelligent. Proverbs 18:13, says, "He who gives an answer before he hears, it is folly and shame to him." To give the impression that you have answers and advice for your mate before you have heard the issue is communication suicide.

President Teddy Roosevelt once became tired of simply smiling at White House receptions. One evening he decided to do an experiment. He wanted to know if anyone was really paying attention. As he shook hands with the guest who walked through the line, he would smile and say, "I murdered my grandmother this morning." Person after person never noticed! Some even said, "Good work, Mr. President" or "How lovely." Genuine listening is so overlooked and so much needed. James 1:19 reminds us to be quick to listen.

We might think in terms of hearing as the process of taking in information while listening is the process of connecting with another person. Hearing another person can inform you, but listening to another person will show you care and want to understand what they are sharing.

Listening is a powerful force in the building of intimacy because it sends the message that you are accepting the other person. A marriage cannot thrive without mutual acceptance. Intimacy cannot grow without it. Communication is one key way we can demonstrate acceptance.

Sharing is the other part of good communication. We have over 600,000 words in our English language. The 500 most frequently used words have a total of 14,000 definitions. From a mathematical standpoint, we have about one chance in 28 of choosing identical meanings for our most frequently used words. Our average speaking rate is around 150 words per minute but our brains can process anywhere from 600 to 1,000 words a minute. We can hear much faster than we can talk. But sharing involves more than just words. Words are symbols of thought that mean something. Words can encourage or they can hurt.

Proverbs 18:21 reminds us that "death and life are in the power of the tongue." Proverbs 15:23 teaches us how important the right words at the right time can be. "How delightful is a timely word."

When our mate shares something critical with us we must be cautious, loving, and honest in our response. It is so easy to defend ourselves or explain ourselves when we feel like we are being criticized. The failure to really communicate can be seen in offering an apology too soon, attacking our spouse, handing out advice, patronizing the other person, or attempting to correct our mate's perception.

Even though words are important and powerful, our touch may send an even stronger message than our words. Physical touch can be a very positive and affirming form of communication. One woman conducted an experiment with some coins in a telephone booth. She deliberately left some change in the coin return of the pay phone. After another person began to use the phone, she approached them and asked if they would give her the coins she had left in the phone. When she only used words, 30 percent of the people gave her the coins. But, when she gently touched the person's arm and used words, 60 percent of the people gave her the coins. A well-timed and appropriate touch can send such a vibrant message to your mate. Touch is free and it can soothe a person better than drugs or alcohol. It can lower your blood pressure. It can relax you. Physical touch is a powerful resource.

Silence is a form of negative communication. It is usually a passive-aggressive approach that is geared more toward defending and punishing than it is to building good will between partners. Sarcasm is a popular expression among many couples. It is the "put down" that can easily damage a relationship.

There are many ways we can share and receive. Our hope for building intimacy through communication is to work at it. We can build the kind of awareness and commitment that focuses on making connections rather than passing time or passing along information. Couples can grow in their communication skills by devoting the time necessary to hone those skills. Messages should be clearly sent. This takes the game playing and guess work out of it. Messages should also be received with understanding. Listening is an art that we must consciously be developing over the span of marriage.

Chapter 9

Money Matters

Sex, in-laws, and money have occupied the top positions as major marital problems. Today, the leading problem in marriage is money. Money matters. It matters how we earn it, how much we earn, how we use it, and if we save it. How a couple handles money is critical to the overall condition of their relationship.

Gottman emphasizes, "Whether their bank account is teeming or they're just scrimping by, many couples confront significant money conflicts. Often such disputes are evidence of a perpetual issue, since money is symbolic of many emotional needs – such as for security and power – and goes to the core of our individual value system."[1]

Good and Godly money management begins with our grace giving to God. Should a Christian tithe? Because we live in the blessing of God's grace, we should give at least a tithe. Our beginning point for managing our money should begin with 10% of our gross income and increase as God prospers us. In Jesus' Sermon on the Mount in Matthew 5-6, He referred to teachings based on the law that were prevalent during those days. In each case, Jesus contrasted that teaching by saying, "but I say to you…." What He said next in every case was more than

101

the Law or their understanding of the Law required. Christians are called to give generously as an expression of worship. II Corinthians 9:6-8 cannot be overlooked by couples who are serious about serving God and responsibly handling their money. "Now this I say, he who sows sparingly will also reap sparingly, and he who sows bountifully will also reap bountifully. Each one must do just as he has purposed in his heart, not grudgingly or under compulsion, for God loves a cheerful giver. And God is able to make all grace abound to you, so that always having all sufficiency in everything, you may have an abundance for every good deed."

Faithful money management reflects the concept that we are not really owners of anything but managers of what God has given us. God is the owner of everything. "The earth is the Lord's, and all it contains, the world, and those who dwell in it" (Psalm 24:1). Our responsibility and privilege as God's people is to be trustworthy with whatever He allows us to manage. The principle is found in I Corinthians 4:2 where Paul writes that "it is required of stewards that one be found trustworthy." It has been preached many times that we cannot out give God. It is true. But our giving to God must not be motivated by some type of investment thinking. When we give money to support the work of God on this planet, we will receive back much more but it might not always be in cold hard cash. The blessings God gives to His faithful stewards may include financial blessings but they will not be limited to that one category. God may choose to bless us in other areas that may be actually more valuable than money.

Many couples enter their marriage already strapped with a large amount of debt. This immediately puts a strain on their relationship in ways they never imagined. The average American spends more than he or she earns in a year. Personal bankruptcies are around 1 ½ million a year. Over 55 million Americans need debt help. The average amount of unpaid credit card debt for families is somewhere between $8,000 and $12,000. Personal debt in the United States is higher than ever before.[2]

Money matters in a marriage because it affects the ways we relate to each other. How money is spent both shapes and reveals the values and feelings of the family system. It takes money to live, but living well is not dependent on a certain amount of money. In the western world particularly, we have a bad habit of loving money. We are a materialistic culture, and we want the things and the comforts money can provide. If we don't have the money available, we simply borrow it. This pattern leads to financial trouble and family problems.

The Bible does not condemn having money, spending money, saving money, or using money. However, the love of money is condemned. I Timothy 6:7-10 reminds us of a sobering reality. "For we have brought nothing into the world, so we cannot take anything out of it either. If we have food and covering, with these we shall be content. But those who want to get rich fall into temptation and a snare and many foolish and harmful desires which plunge men into ruin and destruction. For the love of money is a root of all sorts of evil, and some by longing for it have wandered away from the faith and pierced themselves with many griefs."

Consumer debt in the 1990's was a staggering $800 billion. Now it has surpassed $2 trillion! More and more family income is going to service debt while fewer and fewer families are saving money. This scenario is a recipe for short term stress and long term misery! The tension and bondage that unmanageable debt brings into a couple's life cannot be precisely measured but is reflected in a divorce rate that continues to hover around 50 percent.

Debt is a burden that is draining the emotional energy from millions of families in America. Proverbs

22:7 says, "The rich rules over the poor, And the borrower becomes the lender's slave." Romans 13:8 counsels us, "Owe nothing to anyone except to love one another...." Debt exists when liabilities exceed assets or when what we owe is greater than what we make. It is not wrong to have a mortgage on a home. For most couples owning a home is one of their chief goals. The problem comes when our spending exceeds our income. When we cannot meet our obligations, we have unmanageable debt. A couple can buy something on credit without technically incurring debt. A contract is an agreement to pay back the price of the purchase along with the interest charged. When we do not have the means to do that, we are in the bondage of debt.

It seems that overall, financial counselors are suggesting that housing expenses which would include rent or mortgage payments, property tax, and property insurance should not exceed 28 percent of our gross income. Many recommend that our total debt be no more than 36 percent of our family income. They further counsel us to pay ourselves or save at least 10 percent of our gross income and increase the percentage as we get older and approach retirement.

How much should a couple have in a savings account? Hopefully, we will save as much as we can.

Specifically, we would be wise to have an amount equal to about six months of income. If a job was lost or our family income dropped, we would have enough money available to live while we found a job or made the necessary adjustments in our standard of living. Having that much money in reserve would at least give us time to work out a strategy without intense financial pressure.

Developing and maintaining a family budget is a discipline that pays dividends in many ways. However, most couples who do not have a budget in place would be better served to first list all their current expenditures. Some of the items that would fit into this exercise would be: giving to God's work, mortgage or rent, utilities, groceries, taxes, household and vehicle maintenance, clothes, personal care, health care, insurance, gifts, vacations and trips, investments, recreation, entertainment, and incidental expenses. Your actual list would include many specific items. The list above is more like categories than specific expenditures.

Husbands have a tendency to overspend in the areas of high-tech devices, sports events and equipment, and meals outside the home. Women are more likely to overspend on the kids, clothing, and beauty supplies.

After determining what your actual expenditures are, you can then compare how that relates to your income. If you are spending more than you are making, some hard decisions will need to be made. Husband and wife may then work together to decide what is essential and what can be reduced or eliminated in their current spending patterns. Couples that examine their expenditures and work on a strategy for living within their income do not always find a clear solution, but they almost always see the emotional climate of their relationship changed. They begin to feel more like a team and that helps to reduce the stress that financial pressure has brought to bear on the couple.

From an honest listing of family expenditures comes the process of developing a budget. Different personalities approach budgeting in different ways. The main objective to keep in mind is that you have a plan for living with the money you have available to you. The list of expenditures, which at this point will be modified by eliminating some items and reducing others, can serve as the outline for developing a budget. Adding a miscellaneous item in your budget along with increasing your health care estimate is a good idea. We regularly underestimate how much we spend in these two areas. Including a monthly savings payment is a good item to add to the budget as well. Saving is a good discipline that indicates the presence of wisdom. Proverbs 21:20 says, "There is precious treasure and oil in the dwelling of the wise, but a foolish man swallows it up."

Finally a budget comes into existence. It is a plan for managing our money. A couple should monitor their budget to be sure they are keeping their spending in line with their resources. They should also discuss their financial goals and dreams together. Sharing our perspectives, values, and feelings with our mate helps us to build the kind of togetherness that breeds a sense of confidence, respect, and security.

Even after you have developed a budget that is workable, you may have to deal with the accumulation of debt. The goal would be to work out a plan to pay the interest on the debt and repay the debt as soon as possible. For many couples, seeing a professional financial counselor may be the most beneficial route to take.

Once we have a budget in place and the commitment to live within its parameters, we can then grow in our attitude toward money and things. So many couples get caught in financial difficulties because of impulse buying or purchasing things to gain a perceived status level they think they want. Someone once noted that too many of us "buy things we don't need with money we don't have to impress people we don't even like."

A vehicle is usually a major purchase for the average couple. A vehicle is a necessity for most of us in our mobile society. But, we must understand that a vehicle is always an expense and never an investment. They depreciate rapidly. Generally, a new vehicle purchase is not the best choice. A good used vehicle with low miles is a much better expenditure. Another area in which couples can overspend and buy things they do not need or will not use is at the supermarket. Some general guidelines can help us in this practice: don't shop while you are hungry, use a list, shop only once a week, avoid junk foods, compare products and ounces per container vs. cost, use coupons, look for bargains, and buy non-perishables in quantity when feasible.

Another trap that can easily deceive us and lead us to make some bad buying choices is advertising. By the time the average child graduates from high school, he or she will have seen over 350,000 advertisements. Advertising is big business, and it can be very misleading. It is appealing and enticing. Advertisers are interested in selling products. They are not personally concerned about your financial health. We seldom strongly desire something we have not seen through advertising. If we choose not to look at ads in print or through other mediums, we will spend less.

When it comes to impulse buying, couples need to work together. An excellent tactic is to use the delay principle. After seeing something you feel you must have, wait a day or two before you look at it again. Then, only buy it if you can pay for it and if it fits into your budget or is a mutually agreed upon decision that you can afford.

Credit cards can be a convenient way to make purchases or they can become the devil in disguise. The best way to use credit cards is to pay the balance each month and avoid any interest charges. The worst thing we can do is use a credit card to get us further into debt. Interest payments mount up.

As a couple moves through life, they should be building some type of financial resource for their retirement years. In spite of a variety of options that are available, most of us will have our investments for retirement centered in a few areas: a retirement plan (either private or with our employer), life insurance, savings account, our career, and our home. Many baby boomers will inherit significant sums of money. This generation, characterized by high expectations, must be careful to avoid self-indulgence and plan wisely. The bumper sticker seen on the motor homes of a number of senior citizens across the country is amusing, "I'm spending my children's inheritance." It is a sign of affection and wisdom when we can leave an inheritance for our children and their children. Proverbs 13:22 says, "A good man leaves an inheritance to his children's children...."

As husband and wife enter the empty nest years where the children have moved out and the retirement years are moving in, they can enjoy each other as much as ever if they have adjusted their standard of living leading up to that time.

Husbands and wives are a team. That is clearly evident in the area of finances. When they can use money without it using them, they can continue to build intimacy until death concludes the cycle of their marriage.

Sources Quoted

Chapter One: Designed For Intimacy

1. Howard J. and Charlotte H. Clinebell. The Intimate Marriage (Harper and Row Publishers, New York, New York, 1970) pgs. 29-32

Chapter Three: Personalities At Work

1. Otto Kroeger and Janet M. Theuesen. 16 Ways To Love Your Lover (Delacorte Press, New York, New York, 1994) pp. 24.

Chapter Four: The Influence Of Birth Order

1. Merri Wallace. Birth Order Blues (Henry Holt and Co., New York, New York, 1999) pp. 6.

2. Kevin Leman. The New Birth Order Book (Fleming H. Revell, Grand Rapids, Michigan, 1998) pp. 7.

3. Ibid., p. 217

Chapter Five: Distinctively Male and Female

1. Larry Crabb. Men and Women: Enjoying The Difference (Zondervan Publishing House, Grand Rapids Michigan, 1991) pg. 198, 202.

2. John MacArthur. Different By Design: Discovering God's Will For Today's Man and Woman (Victor Books, Wheaton, Illinois, 1994) pp. 44.

3. Pierce J. Howard. The Owner's Manual For The Brain: Everyday Applications From Mind-Brain Research (Bard Press, Austin, Texas, 2000) pp. 219.

4. John Gray. Men Are From Mars, Women Are From Venus (HarperCollins Publisher, New York, New York, 1992) pgs. 132-133.

5. Willard F. Harley. His Needs, Her Needs: Building An Affair Proof Marriage (Fleming H. Revell Co, Old Tappan, New Jersey, 1986) pp. 41, 10.

6. Deborah Tannen. You Just Don't Understand: Women and Men In Conversation (William Morrow and Co., New York, New York, 1990) pg. 150, 154.

Chapter Six: The Friendship Factor

1. John M. Gottman. The Seven Principles For Making Marriage Work (Crown Publishers, New York, New York, 1999) pp17

2. John M. Gottman. Why Marriages Succeed Or Fail.... And How You Can Make Yours Last (Simon and Schuster Inc., New York, New York, 1994) pg. 69-102.

Chapter Seven: The Sexual Key

1. Archibald Hart. Healing Life's Addictions (Servant Publications, Ann Arbor, Michigan, 1996) pp. 156

2.   Archibald Hart, Catherine Hart Weber, Debra Taylor. The Secrets Of
   Eve: Understanding The Mystery of Female Sexuality (Word Publishing,
     Nashville, Tennessee, 1998) pp. 43.

3. Sallie Foley, Sally A. Kope, Dennis P. Sugrue. Sex Matters For Women:
    A Complete Guide To Taking Care Of Your Sexual Self (The Guilford
     Press, New York, 2002), pp. 75

4.   Ibid., pp. 77-78, 205

Chapter Nine: Money Matters

1.   Gottman.   The Seven Principles For Making Marriage Work, pp. 194.

2.   Financial Planning Association Survey of 189 Financial Planners, 2006

About The Author

James Rudy Gray is a pastor and counselor. He and his wife Anne have been married over 30 years. They have three adult daughters: Becky, Katy, and Cindy. Rudy is a graduate of Anderson, Southern Wesleyan, and Liberty Universities. He has also earned two degrees from Luther Rice Seminary. He writes for two publications: **The Baptist Courier** and **Pulpit Helps.** He has served as a trustee for Anderson University, The Baptist Courier, and New Orleans Baptist Theological Seminary.

Rudy and Anne have conducted marriage enrichment retreats for churches and groups for over 20 years. Anne teaches math, children's Sunday School, and sings in the choir at church. Rudy has been named to Who's Who In Religion in America, Who's Who Among Human Service Professionals, and Outstanding Young Men of America. He is a member of the American Association of Christian Counselors and is a National Certified Counselor.

This is his fourth book.